My
SHIELD
THE POWER THAT PROTECTS US
FROM THE ASSAULTS OF THE ENEMIES
FEHINTOLA AYOOLA

MY SHIELD

Copyright @ 2020 by Fehintola M. Ayoola

ISBN: 9798588984935

**Published By:
Royal Trumpet Publication,
Sure Mercies Ministries**

For more information about Sure Mercies Ministries

visit suremerciesministries.org or

call 832-328-3800

King's Daughter @ suremerciesministries.org

FEHINTOLA M. AYOOLA

P.O. BOX 721615

HOUSTON Texas 77272

FEHINTOLA AYOOLA

This book is a Gift

____

From

____

To

____

Date

MY SHIELD

Dedication

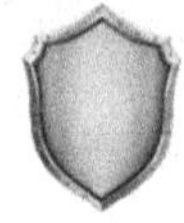

With great joy I dedicate this book to my daughter, Toluwanimi and my son, Emmanuel.

I am confident the almighty God will reward them for their loving and faithful commitment to the service of God's Kingdom and their understanding to us.

"Our Shield is with God, who saves the upright in heart." (Psalm 7:10 ESV)

Acknowledgement

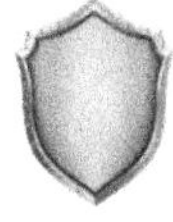

I am eternally grateful for the Trinity: The almighty God for His mercy, grace, and love towards me; The LORD Jesus, my savior, for the salvation of my soul, whose love has transformed my life; and the sweet Holy Spirit for divine inspiration and help to write this book.

I also want to thank God for my husband, Toyin Ayoola, for his love, care, and support. His mentorship has really helped in God's assignment for my life. And God's ark, Toluwanimi and Emmanuel, the two of you have been a great encouragement and support, thank you for your understanding. I pray to God to continue to be our shield.

I am grateful for all of you.

Table Of Content

Introduction

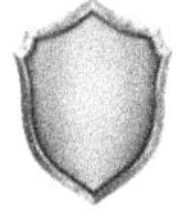

According to Strong's Concordance, the Hebrew word for Shield is *"Magen"*, which means a protective armor. It is used for protection or as a treasure of war.

A shield is something or someone that provides protection from danger or risk. Regardless of the type of shield or what is being shielded, a shield's major purpose is to protect, guard, and defend against incoming danger, risk, or unpleasant experience. For example, the purpose of a pupil in the human eyes is to control the rate at which the light is let into the eye. When exposed to sunlight, the pupil shrinks to protect "the sensitive photoreceptors in our retina", thereby protecting the eye from damage. Even with the provision of natural protection, we still have all kinds of sunglasses that serve as a shield providing protection for our eyes against sun rays.

> *Without the help of supreme power that can only be found in God Almighty, one will be a prey for the devil and his assaults.*

Daily we are faced with the battles of our lives, ranging from spiritual, physical, emotional, mental, and moral battles. Sometimes even our dreamland has become a battle ground, except when we have the almighty God as our shield, victory will become something attainable. Many have suffered loss because they have faced their life's battles unshielded or not properly covered. Without the help of supreme power that can only be found in God Almighty, one will be a prey for the devil and his assaults.

This Book My Shield provides you with the different types of shields that have been provided for us in Christ. And if we wear our shields properly, we are sure of victory, for our LORD Jesus Christ has already won the battle. This is not an abstract book but an experience. With God as my shield, I have seen Him fighting and winning my battle time after time, and I can boldly declare by His mercy and grace, that I am a woman who always wins. Therefore, you don't have to lose again or struggle in life's battleground. If you have God, MY Shield, you are destined to win!

GOD's SHIELD

When we have the almighty God as our shield, victory will become something attainable.

CHAPTER ONE

God's Shield

*I*n the Bible, apostle Paul commands us as Christians to ***"put on the full armor of God so we can stand against the evil days" (Ephesian 6:13).***

We are living in the evil days, and Satan and his agents are launching their attacks more than ever before; we must not let down our guard.

Like in football, the team on defense protects their end zone from the opponents trying to score. Just like in sports, no matter how the defensive team guards against the opponent from scoring points, we still see the opposing team managing to score, especially if they have good players. "Except God watches over the house", the psalmist writes in the scripture, *"the watchman watches in vain."* God is the ultimate and only dependable defender against anything that might want to invade our life.

Dr. Martin Luther King Jr says it best, *"A safe stronghold our God is still. A trusty Shield and weapon."*

When God is our shield, absolutely nothing can come through Him to us unless He permits it. He is an impenetrable force against any intrusion of our life.

You, Lord, Are A Shield About Me

But you, LORD, are a shield around me, my glory, the One who lifts my head high.
(Psalm 3:3 NLT)

When faced with situations in life where fear creeps in, we should not forget who our shield is. In the above scripture, situations have transpired in the life of David and they were unpalatable circumstances. His son Absalom has taken over the kingdom and, as if that wasn't enough, he was running for his life. He met with the Benjamites who resorted to physical violence, throwing rocks at him, and accused him, saying that he deserved what was happening to him. David refused to let his few followers defend him and he wouldn't defend himself either *(2 Samuel 16:5-7)*, but he looked back and confidently declared who his shield was.

Though enemies were increasing left, right, center, and the voices that were approaching dictated a state of helplessness for David, he assured himself in this situation, ***"But you, LORD"*** *not man, now, before, and forever are a shield around me* - a shield against physical or spiritual rocks.

If you're being shielded, you cannot be seen or hurt because there is protection. God as our shield is providing protection for us all around. He is our buckler, covering, wall of defense, security, a shelter and support (bearing all the weight). God is our assistance: the one who enables us to function.

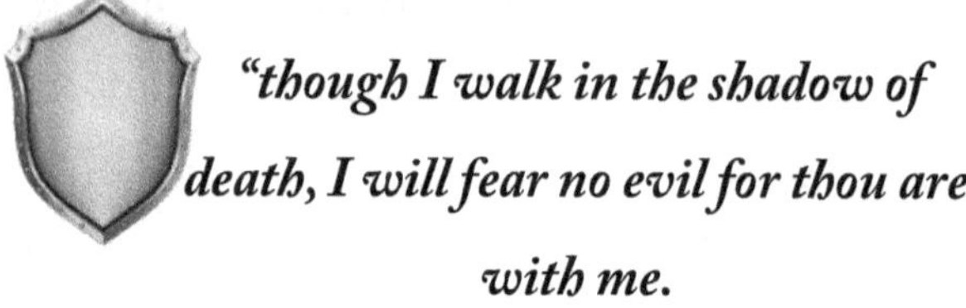

"though I walk in the shadow of death, I will fear no evil for thou are with me.

Having God as your shield means you are secured, free from danger and threat. I am not saying you will not see, hear, or feel threatened, but it will do you no harm. David said, "though I walk in the shadow of death, I will fear no evil for thou are with me." God will protect you from all forms of attacks in Jesus' mighty name.

No Fear When GOD Is Your Shield

"Sometime later, the LORD spoke to Abram in a vision and said to him, '

Do not be afraid, Abram, for I will protect you, and your reward will be great"

(Genesis 15:1 NLT).

Abram had just finished a battle with five kings; he rescued his nephew Lot and brought back all that the enemy took including Lot's family and others. The Lord appeared to him in Genesis chapter 15 verse 1,

"Do not be afraid, Abram, I am your shield, your very great reward" (NKV).

The LORD assured him no matter the threat or fear from the defeated kings, He will shield Abram and be his defense. God promised Abram he need not worry about the counterattack from the kings he had just defeated, for He will be the bulwark for him - a defensive wall against his enemy.

It is worthy of note that Abram could not have defeated the five kings with all their armies, weapons, and chariots, if God had not been his shield. Just as Moses put it,

"How could one man chase a thousand, or two put ten thousand to flight, unless their Rock had sold them, unless the Lord had given them up?" (Deuteronomy 32:30 NIV).

The almighty God has given the five kings up and that's why Abraham and his servants could defeat them without lifting a weapon. This is what will be your portion also; you will not have to raise a finger against the troops coming against you for God has given them up and they are defeated in Jesus' name.

Like the wall surrounds Jerusalem, the almighty God surrounds us His children, and we shall not be moved by the enemy's threat. Even Satan knows that when the almighty God is your shield you are untouchable for him. He told God when God was boasting about Job, that Job only reverences God because He built a hedge roundabout all that he had *(Job 1:10). Though the reason given by Satan for Job's reference was incorrect, he was right about one thing: God truly had a hedge round about Job and all he owned.* It is my prayer that God Almighty will be your shield, defense, the bulwark, the wall that protects you from all the assaults of the enemy.

GOD, MY COVERING FROM THE STORMS OF LIFE

No one is exempted from the storm of life. But if God is your shield, you are covered and sheltered

CHAPTER TWO

God, My Covering From The Storms Of Life

"The Lord will wash away the filth of the women of Zion; he will cleanse the bloodstains from Jerusalem by a spirit of judgment and a spirit of fire. 5 Then the Lord will create over all of Mount Zion and over those who assemble there a cloud of smoke by day and a glow of flaming fire by night; over everything the glory will be a canopy. 6 It will be a shelter and shade from the heat of the day, and a refuge and hiding place from the storm and rain" (Isaiah 4:4-6).

The LORD our God is a righteous judge, He will not cast away the perfect man. He is a present help, but know this, He will not help the evildeors. In chapter one, we see how God was able to help Abram - the perfect man - against the battle of Kings that stormed his nephew Lot in the land of Sodom, where he, his wives, children, and all his possessions were taken away. The storm of life doesn't announce before knocking on our door. It comes, to the rich, the poor, the strong, and the weak; no one is exempted from the storm of life. But if God is your shield, you are covered and sheltered for He will surround you and all yours with a cloud of smoke by day and glow of flaming fire by night. Over all that is yours, the glory of His presence will be a canopy, protecting you from the storms of life.

Although God is the canopy in which we hide from the rain, heat, and storms of life, we must be in tune with Him. We must stay connected and obey all His instructions. He knows all things and can do all things. God cares and wants to protect us from all imminent danger. He will either warn us or prepare us for what is coming, but if we choose not to obey, we most likely suffer for it unless there is divine intervention.

Noah's Ark

The story of Noah's ark is a very good example of a man in tune with his God. Noah was obedient and a man of faith. He was told by God to build an Ark because there was going to be a rain that would destroy everything on earth. The only things that would be protected and safe from the flood would be what was on the Ark. Noah believed and obeyed God by building the Ark *(Genesis 6:22)*.

Let's imagine Noah heard God but refused to yield to the instruction of building the Ark; he would have been destroyed with the rest of the people that the flood swept away. It is good that Noah obeyed God, because the ark eventually served as a shield for him, his family, and the animals. Although it was scary and threatening to hear the noise of the rain, thunder, and the flood for forty days, God shielded him using the ARK. For 150 days after the rain had stopped, God protected, provided for, and preserved everything in the Ark. God wants to be your shield, but you must be in tune with him and be obedient to His instructions.

God's instructions might look and sound foolish to us, but we must choose to be obedient. Others might tell us it doesn't sound right or look good, but ultimately you were the one that heard God's voice and the one who needs to acknowledge him as your shield; you must disregard what others are saying and follow his voice.

God's instructions might look and sound foolish to us, but we must choose to be obedient.

It is important that you know how God speaks to

you and understand his voice from amongst other noises. Nowadays, we are too busy, and God is speaking louder than before. I pray that you will hear him. He said, my sheep hear me and the voice of a stranger they will not hear.

"The priesthood of God is a shield. It is a shield against the evils of the world. That shield needs to be kept clean; otherwise our vision of our purpose and the dangers around us will be limited."

~ James E. Faust

For us to hear God, our relationship must not be strained. Our antennae must be on and anything that will hinder us from hearing God must be removed. Clean your ear of every ear salve that can block it from hearing the whispering of God's instruction.

In that storm or whatever situation you may be in, abide in GOD and be obedient to his commands, and I assure you the storm will pass, the rain will stop, and you will be protected from the flood and covered from the rain, for He will be all you need. He has promised to be with us when we pass through the waters and through the rivers - we will not be swept over, neither will the fire burn us when we walk through it. The most important thing is for us to be sure that we are in tune with His Spirit and be obedient to His leading.

Isaiah 37:33-35: "Therefore thus says the Lord concerning the king of Assyria: He shall not come into this city or shoot an arrow there or come before it with a shield or cast up a siege mound against it. 34 By the way that he came, by the same he shall return, and he shall not come into this city, declares the Lord. 35 For I will defend this city to save it, for my own sake and for the sake of my servant David."

Confession is Possession: Declare it with me:

I confess that the almighty GOD is a shield about

me, my home, my children, my marriage, my finance, my health, my business, my ministry, and my family in Jesus' name. No arrow, flood, or storm of life will come near us in Jesus' mighty name. As the lion or the young lion roaring on his prey, when a multitude of shepherds are called forth against him, he will not be afraid of their voice, nor abase himself for the noise of them; so shall the LORD of hosts come down to fight for mount Zion and for the hill thereof. As birds flying, so will the LORD of hosts defend Jerusalem. In defending also, he will deliver it and passing over he will preserve it. My life and all mine are hiding under the shadow of the Almighty. We are covered in Jesus' name. Amen.

THE WORD OF GOD IS A SHIELD

The word of God is reliable, dependable, and sure.

CHAPTER THREE

The Word Of God Is A Shield

Reading, listening, and memorizing the word of God has a great advantage. Though we might not need the word at that moment, when we need it, it will come out as a shield ready to defend us whether it is for our health, marriage, children, or career.

The wisest man that ever lived, Solomon, wrote,

"Every word of God is pure: he is a shield unto them that put their trust in him"

(Proverbs 30:5).

The word of God is reliable, dependable, and sure.

Kingdoms rise and fall, generations come and go but, the word of God remains the same and has been passed down to many generations as a shield to hold onto in all seasons of life. You can lay hold on the word and, regardless of how long, it will not fail. God honors His word more than His name.

Job, a rich and God-fearing man, observed the world we are living in and he said,

"For affliction does not come forth from the dust, nor does trouble spring forth from the ground. For man is born for trouble, [As naturally] as sparks fly upward"

(Job 5:6-7 AMP).

There have been times I have been in deadly, fearful, and scary situations and I didn't know how things would turn out. But one thing I did during those times was to keep my confidence in God and His word, and that has always been my help.

My trust in His word is that He will not fail. Like the writer of an old hymn put it:
"Tis so sweet to trust in Jesus,
Just to take Him at His word;
Just to rest upon His promise;
Just to know, Thus saith the Lord."

Being able to hear God matters when we are faced with fearful situations in life. I remember that then my marriage was about three years old and it looked like it was about to end. My husband had just been diagnosed with cancer of the blood - leukemia. It was one of the acute ones, a cancer of the blood-forming tissues, including bone marrow, hindering the body's ability to fight infection. In one of our visits to his primary physician, his doctor analyzed how the next few years would be, and it was not promising anything good.

As a matter of fact, we met an uncle of his that was a medical doctor and very experienced; he also told us that is was going to be very rough and he wasn't sure if my husband would survive. I was terrified and overwhelmed, but I also remembered that the promises of God says yes and amen. His plan is of good and not evil, to give hope and an anticipated end. Though doctors couldn't promise us anything positive, I chose to believe God's word; I chose to put my ultimate trust in His words that cannot fail.

The Bible says

> *"Some trust in chariots, and some in horses: but we will remember the name of the Lord our God. They are brought down and fallen but we are risen and stand upright"*
>
> *(Psalm 20:7-8).*

Just as doctors predicted, things were falling apart. Right after he did the bone marrow test, he could not walk or sleep. The fear of death was all over, and the news we were getting was threatening. I remember vividly, one faithful morning, after we had finished our morning devotion, the word of God to us from the book of *Acts 18:9-10:*

> *"Then spake the Lord to Paul in the night by a vision, Be not afraid, but speak, and hold not thy peace: For I am with thee, and no man shall set on thee to hurt thee: for I have much people in this city."*

I want to tell you that, before the diagnosis and up until now, we are fervent Christians. I know my stance before God, but just as I mentioned in the previous chapter, the storms of life come knocking when you least expect and no matter who you are, a believer or a nonbeliever, rich or poor, weak or strong, you are not exempted. My husband and I were among a small group that interceded for our senior pastor at the time, and we were also members of the church intercessory and drama group. We are serving and occupying for the LORD as he has commanded. Yet the news came of the deadly diagnosis. I was very scared and wondered how we are going to make it through. Our children were very young at the time and our immediate family was far away.

Though I had the word of God that said do not fear, the situation was dreadful and very scary, and the truth is I was afraid. My husband had swollen overnight to three times his former size. And on getting to the hospital it was like I was watching a movie - things just started happening around me. They immediately prepared him for the chemotherapy and had several tests done. Before the results of the test came, he was unconscious and so many things were going on in my head.

Things were just happening fast paced, forms were given to me to be signed, questions were being asked for a man that has never been this sick in his life. I didn't know how we got there within a week. Still unconscious, they started dialysis. The result came in that it was not cancer of the blood, not leukemia, but still he was very sick.

Amidst this, I remembered this word in the book of *Acts 18:7*

> ***"Do not be afraid—I am with you, no man shall set on you to hurt you."***

My instinct was "God I am already hurting, and I don't know what to do."

I heard the voice of God say you don't know what it means to be hurt - I am saying there will be no hurt, no pain, or injury. I was hearing the word, but everything seemed opposite. I had to look up what no hurt meant. It means no pain, no scar, and no injury, and in my spirit I accepted, forever O Lord thy word is true. We may feel fear and hear threatening news, but God's words promise no hurt. God's word is final authority over any situation if we will choose to believe Him.

I chose to believe God's word over the doctor's reports. Prayers were being made on our behalf. God raised up people to stand in the gap and help in different ways. The word of God was my greatest weapon during that season. His word was a shield roundabout us, and though my husband was very close to death, God saved him.

Today, if you happened to meet my husband, and he didn't tell you that he was on life support for almost three months, went through dialysis due to multiple organ failure, with his whole skin peeling times without number, you would never know. God has fully restored him, and he is healthy. But it is very true, he went through all that and more, but God promised no hurt, no scar, and no pain. His muscles collapsed making his left side not function well, and he was expected to be in a wheelchair for life, but God said there will be no scar and now he is walking with no assistance. The word of God is pure, a shield to us who choose to trust in Him.

Regardless of what you are going through in life, choose to seek God and know his word over your situation. His word prevails over attacks, sickness, lack, afflictions; no power can stand against the power of God's word. At his rebuke, mountains skip like rams and melt like wax. I remember, every morning during that season of our life, I would give my husband the word though he could not respond, but just like the doctors and nurses came to check his vitals and pass medication through drips, I confessed the word of life (God) over him and declared that the counsel of God alone will stand. Today we are a testimony that the word of God is a shield to those who trust Him.

THE NAME OF
THE LORD,
MY STRONG TOWER

The name of the LORD is a strong tower, whenever we run to him as children of God, we find safety.

CHAPTER FOUR

The Name Of The Lord, My Strong Tower

The name of the Lord is a strong tower; The righteous runs to it and is safe and set on high [far above evil] (Proverbs 18:10).

The name of the LORD is a strong tower, whenever we run to him as children of God, we find safety.

The name of LORD was mostly revealed amid the time of Israel's need. Moses' encounter with the LORD at the burning bush was real, but his fear of Pharaoh and the Jews didn't allow him to accept the call immediately until God revealed himself as I AM that I AM.

> *"And Moses said unto God, Who am I, that I should go unto Pharaoh, and that I should bring forth the children of Israel out of Egypt? And he said, Certainly I will be with thee; and this shall be a token unto thee, that I have sent thee: When thou hast brought forth the people out of Egypt, ye shall serve God upon this mountain. And Moses said unto God, Behold, when I come unto the children of Israel, and shall say unto them, The God of your fathers hath sent me unto you; and they shall say to me, What is his name? what shall I say unto them? And God said unto Moses, I Am That I Am: and he said, thus shalt thou say unto the children of Israel, I Am hath sent me unto you" (Exodus 3:11-14 KJV).*

The name "I AM THAT I AM" served as confidence for Moses to embark on the greatest assignment of his life, to deliver Israel from their bondage in Egypt. Indeed, I AM had sent him and His presence was a great shield for Moses when standing face to face with Pharaoh. Moses, once a fugitive, entered Egypt with confidence in the name of the LORD Jehovah - I AM THAT AM. Pharaoh could not arrest him, and he accomplished his assignment by bringing the Israelites out of slavery. God's name is a strong tower.

God's name I AM was all that Moses needed. Indeed, God was I AM, all Moses needed as he took the journey to Egypt and even as they left Egypt for the promise land. I AM was water from the rock when the Israelites were thirsty, and the manna that fell from heaven in the wilderness where there were no grocers from which to purchase food.

> *"Yea, forty years didst thou sustain them in the wilderness, so that they lacked nothing; their clothes waxed not old, and their feet swelled not" (Nehemiah 9:21 KJV).*

God was their everything - I AM THAT AM. It is my prayer that God will be your I AM THAT AM - *He will be everything you need you will never lack for anything, and he will surely sustain you in every season of life.*

The Name of the LORD is a Shield to Us as Servants of God

The name of the LORD is powerful and several times God has revealed himself to the people in the Old Testament introducing Himself with different names. These names today give us comfort and help us in our own time of need, as he did for the patriarchs of old. In this chapter, I am going to mention a few of the names that I personally have experienced and which have been a great shield for me.

JEHOVAH ELYON – "God Most High"
The most exalted, the one that has the final say,

the final authority over all. David understood this very well; though he was being hunted by King Saul he said in Psalm 7:10,

"My shield is God Most High."

Saul tried so many times to waste David's life, but God Most High was his shield; he would have been pinned on the wall with a javelin, but God shielded him, and he escaped.

Saul proposed that he would not kill David but instead planned to make David fall by the hand of the Philistines *(1 Samuel 18:17- 25)*. He planned to give him his daughter as a wife and find ways to destroy him, yet David escaped.

No matter how men plot against you, if God Most High is your shield they will always fail, and their plans will never see the light of day over you. I know that the Lord God Most High is my shield from the mission of the enemy - to steal, to kill, and destroy. If God has not been my shield, the enemy would have accomplished his three missions, but to God be the glory the enemy has and will always fail.

God has spoken that David will be Israel's next King, though Saul could not comprehend or see it happening. But because David's shield was the righteous judge, David reigned. You too will reach God's destination for your life; Satan will not have the last say over you. Left to the enemy, he was out to steal my joy, kill my husband, and destroy my marriage, but we made God our shield. God's words prevailed and the enemy was defeated. Over all that God has committed to your hand, he will always have the last say. He is the God most high - our Shield.

Make This Declaration With Me:

My shield is God Most High, therefore every attack, retaliation, arrow, or anything the enemy has planned against me will be of no effect. It will backfire against the enemy in Jesus' mighty name. Every evil net spread for me will be in vain; the enemy will fall into the pit they have dug for *me. Because the LORD Most High is my shield, my accusers will perish in shame; those who want to hurt me will be covered with scorn and disgrace. As for me, the Most High is MY shield; I will always hope in God my shield. I will praise you more and more, continual praise to my shield and defense **(PSALM 7:13;15 Proverbs 1:17-18)**.*

JEHOVAH SHALOM – "God our Peace"

The name of God reveals his character. The LORD our God is one, regardless of the situation in which we may find ourselves, it does not change God. He is the same yesterday, today, and forever.

The Lord our peace, was the name of God revealed to Gideon during Israel's most difficult time. They were under the oppression of Midianites. They were forced to hide in caves because the enemy had taken away all their food and livestock. So, to survive, they hid themselves to keep the little they had left.

It was in this situation God found Gideon, the

answer to Israel's cry for deliverance. But Gideon felt he was not adequate and couldn't be the one for the assignment, since he came from the least of the families in Israel - Manasseh. God assured him of His presence, although he could not comprehend that God was with them. I want to submit to us that every time we have an issue, it doesn't mean we have lost the presence of God.

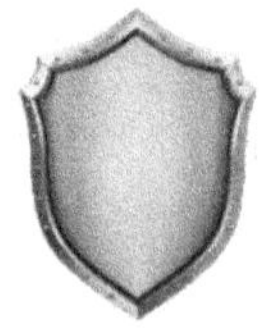 *It's the character of our God that when we seek him, we will find him.*

Although it's true that Israel lost the presence of God because of their disobedience and that God had given them over to the enemy, at this moment, God already answered their cry for help and had come down to help them. It's the character of our God that when we seek him, we will find him. God assured Gideon of His presence in his life and that he would be used to destroy the Midianites. To ensure it was indeed God talking with him, Gideon built an altar and made a sacrifice; his sacrifice was accepted, and this gave him peace. He proceeded to call God "The LORD is Peace."

Gideon was yet to embark in the battle against the Midianites, not knowing what would happen, but he had peace in God who appeared to him and appointed him. In the battle of life, we may pray to God to help us and the answer might not come directly as we desire, but God will give us peace as we go through it.

We will be sure that He is in control and all will be well. This was my case in 2002; there wasn't an immediate healing, but through the process God was with us and give us peace that all will be well. *Jeremiah 29:11* promised that God's thoughts

toward us are thoughts of peace, and not of evil, to give us a desired end.

If we know the expected end and the one who promised us, we will have peace of mind. I implore you to seek to know God and his promises and this will give you peace in every situation.

JEHOVAH SHAMMAH - "The LORD is There"

"And the name of the city from that time on will be: the Lord is there" (Ezekiel 48:35).

Like the children of Israel, we as the children of God have come out of our Egypt, which is sin. We have been through the wilderness, fought the Amalekites, defeated the Midianites, seen the wall of Jericho fall, witnessed Jordan driven back and, to God be the glory, are entering the promise land. Having been through many troubles and threats, I can boldly say we are like the bush that was on fire but not consumed because the LORD was there. He has promised to be with us always and even to the end *(Mathew 28:19-20).*

God did not abandon Jerusalem or leave it in ruins but restored it back again and again. Truly the LORD IS THERE.

God has and will always be there, in your family,

your church, and your businesses to rule and to govern, to protect and to defend. He promised to be near to them that call upon His name. This has been my experience and can be yours too if you decided to the join the camp of the almighty God. He is a present help in the time of trouble *(Psalm 46:1).*

I pray that God will shelter you with His presence and no one will have any cause to ask you of your God. Your testimonies will be of a truth, God is with us.

THE HOUSE OF GOD IS A SHIELD, THE DWELLING PLACE OF THE ALMIGHTY

No matter the offense, if people could just get to the sanctuary and lay hold of the altar, they would be safe.

CHAPTER FIVE

The House Of God Is A Shield, The Dwelling Place Of The Almighty

Even the sparrow has found a home, And the swallow a nest for herself, where she may lay her young— Even Your altars, O LORD of hosts, My King and my God (

Psalm 84:3 NKJV).

In this time that nowhere is safe to be, our world has changed. Someone can enter church and kill because of a difference in religion. This was not so during Biblical times. No matter the offense or the difference, if people could just get to the sanctuary and lay hold of the altar, they would be safe. The altar is a place of refuge and when you hold onto the horn on the altar, it represents appealing to God for mercy and running into the house of God for refuge.

This was the case of Adonijah after he had set himself as King while David was still living. Thank God for the prophet Nathan, because David at this time was very old and had no knowledge of what was happening, and God had already appointed Solomon to be King David's successor. After David declared Solomon king, Adonijah was afraid for his life, but ran to the house of God and held onto the horn and was pardoned.

Now Adonijah was afraid of Solomon; so, he arose, and went and took hold of the horns of the altar. And it was told Solomon, saying, "Indeed Adonijah is afraid of King Solomon; for look, he has taken hold of the horns of the altar, saying, 'Let King Solomon swear to me today that he will not put his servant to death with the sword.'" So, King Solomon sent them to bring him down from the altar. And he came and fell down before King Solomon; and Solomon said to him,

"Go to your house" (1 Kings 1:50-51 & 53).

Regardless of what is happening all around now, I still want you to know that the House of the LORD, the dwelling place of the Almighty, is a shield against the enemy's attacks. As the psalmist said, *"how lovely is your dwelling place, almighty God."* And the popular *Psalm 91, "he that dwell in the shelter (house) of the Most High will rest in the shadow of the Almighty."* The LORD will be your refuge, fortress and shield from the snare of enemies and deadly pestilence.

The house of God is the church of God that has been bought with a price - the blood of Jesus and the Spirit of God is a Witness. Because of the blood of Jesus shed for His saint no plague can come near us *(Exodus 12:13)*.

In the house of God, when we cry out for mercy,

we receive mercy, and forgiveness of our sins from the LORD of the house *(Read 1 Kings. 8:22-61).*

A House or Dwelling Place of God

It is true that God is everywhere, but God's name and the manifestation of His presence is not everywhere. This is the trick of Satan in this end time. Listen to the prayer of Solomon, ***"May your eyes be open toward this temple night and day, this place of which you said, 'My Name shall be there,'*** so that you will hear the prayer your servant prays toward this place." God will only hear if He is there. It is my prayer that God will be wherever life takes you. You and yours will experience His glorious presence at your family altar. Regardless of where you are, the most important thing is for God to be there.

I understand the word of God where the Lord Jesus talked to the Samaritan woman, that the time is coming when you will worship the Father neither on this mountain nor in Jerusalem. God is a Spirit and seeks worshippers who will worship him in spirit and truth. I join Solomon to ask *"will God really dwell on earth? The heaven of heavens cannot contain him... how much less our Cathedral, the big Auditoriums, and sanctuary built to his name."* But he promised to be where His name shall be. No matter how big, or how beautiful or costly the auditorium may be, without God's presence it is just a house, not His dwelling. God's presence is where we gather as His children and that is what makes the difference.

Are You Dwelling In The House of God?

We will enjoy God's blessing of protection if only we are dwelling in His house. The story of the prodigal son, the child that took his inheritance and squandered it, is an amazing story. It shows how we as Christians think, which is to say that we want God's blessing but on our own terms. We can learn from the prodigal son. At the time he left his father, though he had his blessing, he was no longer dwelling with the father. You may have all the blessings but lack his presence, protection, or shield. The lack of his father's (God's) presence reduced the prodigal son and eventually he lost everything. He had to come back to the house for his father (God) to be restored.

Many of God's children are no more abiding with him, and yet we want his blessing, we want him to be our shield. The LORD Jesus said,

> *"if ye abide in me, and my words abide in you, ye shall ask what ye will, and it shall be done unto you" (John 15:7).*

The prodigal son could have sent someone to his father to plead for help on his behalf. But he arose and went to the house, where he was welcome and celebrated. The Father loves us to come to His dwelling place, His arms are open wide to welcome us. Oh, that we may see what we are missing when we are far away from the Father.

Many that have been fervent for the LORD have allowed little breakthroughs to take them away from the Father's presence. The children that they waited for now occupy them that they cannot come to study the word in His presence again. The jobs and businesses they prayed to be successful are time-consuming, and God should understand. Gradually, they stop coming to His house - after all God is everywhere and I can call on him whenever I have time. We forget the word of the apostle,

"Not forsaking the assembling of ourselves together, as the manner of some is; but exhorting one another: and so much the more, as ye see the day approaching"

(Hebrews 10:25).

The only way to keep the blessing - and keep increasing in the blessing - is when we abide in Him. He will not only protect us but protect all he has blessed us with. "Blessed and greatly favored are those who dwell in Your house and Your presence; They will be singing Your praises all the day long" (Psalm 84:4). It is my prayer that continually you will sing the praise of our God -

let there be no break in your relationship with him - abide and dwell in His house.

PRAYER IS A SHIELD

*As great as God is, He still needs
our permission to execute power on earth.*

CHAPTER SIX

Prayer Is A Shield

"God does nothing but by prayer, and everything with it." —*John Wesley*

Prayer is the outcry of a man's heart to God. It opens the door to the greatest power in our life. Prayer moves the hand of God and changes things. There is a saying I believe: God will not do anything but will do everything if we can only find time to pray.

God has delegated the authority to rule and reign on the earth to mankind. As great as God is, He still needs our permission to execute power on earth. If we were more aware of the power of prayer, we would devote more time to prayer in our life. God's anything is your everything, when you ask Him in prayer and in faith.

Talking about prayer as a shield, God expresses his greatest burden through the mouth of His Prophet Ezekiel.

> *"And I sought for a man among them, that should make up the hedge, and stand in the gap before me for the land, that I should not destroy it: but I found none"* *(Ezekiel 22:30).*

Our prayer will protect our family, deliver our city, and save our nation. One person's prayer can serve as a safeguard for a missionary in the mission field, rescue a lost child, or save souls that are perishing. God is still searching for people like Abraham that will stand in the gap for nations that are doomed for destruction, like Sodom and Gomorrah. It was Abraham's prayer that saved Lot and his family from being destroyed in Sodom and Gomorrah.

The iniquity of the land was great and God's judgment was to be poured on them, but due to a man's intercession God saved a family that should have perished. The Bible in Genesis 19:29 says,

> *"So God heeded Abraham's plea and kept Lot safe, removing him from the maelstrom of death that engulfed the cities" (TLB).*

Abraham's prayer saved his nephew from destruction; our prayers are a shield and have the power to avert evil.

The life of Simon Peter, one of Christ's disciples, would have been wasted if prayer was not being made on his behalf in the church while he was kept in prison. King Herod, the great enemy of the gospel, had just killed James and, seeing no one to question him, proceeded to seize Peter and planned to kill him.

Thank God the rest of the disciples didn't question Herod, however they made demand on their God and He saved Peter. God answers the prayer of His people as He promised in 1 Chronicles 7:14:

> *"If my people, which are called by my name, shall humble themselves, and pray, and seek my face, and turn from their wicked ways; then will I hear from heaven, and will forgive their sin, and will heal their land."*

As one of God's generals Oswald Chambers said,

> *"it is not the length of the time we give to a thing that matters but whether the time we give opens the door to the greatest power in our life."*

Prayer is a power that we have as believers and if we will take time to petition heaven, we will experience the supernatural power of God. It will alter us and alter the things around us. Instead of worrying about the situation, lets pray about it,

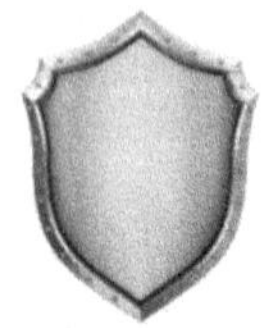

> *"for one minute in prayer will put God's decree at work."*

Redemption has given us access to the throne of

Grace and God answers prayers on the ground of redemption.

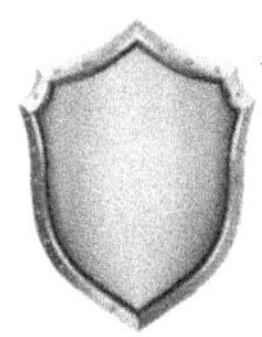

Prayer is your shield as a believer against the assault of the devil in your life and your family.

Robert Liardon had this to say about the life of a "man of healing", John G. Lake, who through his lifestyle of righteousness produced victory in every situation. At his memorial service this was said about him, "Dr. Lake came to Spokane. He found us in sin. He found us in sickness. He found us in poverty of Spirit. He found us in despair but revealed to us such of Christ as we had never dreamed of knowing this side of heaven. We thought the victory was over there, but Dr. Lake revealed to us that victory was here." He is a man that through the power of redemption took his place and changed the nations for God. Through the power of prayer, many experienced healings in John G. Lake ministries, including his siblings and wife.

If You Will Pray, God Will Heal

When we stand on the finished work of Christ and pray, Satan will not have the last word in our life. This was the testimony of John G. Lake when his sister was afflicted with an illness. The sickness was so serious that she was unconscious and without pulse. When John saw her, he was moved with compassion and said, "she must not die! I will not have it." Out of his heart cry and hatred for death and sickness, the Spirit of God stirred up in him and he called upon God in prayer. He also requested for another man of faith to joined him in a prayer of agreement.

In his letter to the man he said, "my sister has apparently died, but my Spirit will not let her go. I believe if you will pray, God will heal her." And his friend John Alexander Dowie replied, "Hold on to God. I am praying. She will live." Together they poured their heart in prayer to God from different places on behalf of his sister. He rebuked the attack of the enemy and the power of death in the name of Jesus Christ. According to the story, in less than an hour, his sister revived totally. This same thing happened to his wife. He is a man that will let God, not Satan, have the last word. It is by prayer that God alone will have the last word over all that God has entrusted to you.

By the special grace of God, I believe strongly that if we pray and let God act, circumstances in our life will have no option but to bow to the name of our Lord Jesus Christ. I know what it means to have men and women of faith join hands with you in your hour of need. I remember when my husband was diagnosed with cancer of the blood, I had a woman that would come to my house every morning to agree with me in prayer; rebuking the spirit of sickness and death and standing in agreement on the word of God. More so, many people came to the hospital chapel to pray for us. Prayers were continuously made on his behalf. Thank God, He heard and answered. I am eternally grateful to God and everyone that agreed with me in faith. Like John G. Lake's words, my husband had apparently died, but we refused to let him go. For God said he will not die but live to declare His glory and God's words prevailed over him. He alone be glorified!

I challenge you to explore the power within you. The power of prayer can save your family, take back what the enemy has stolen, break the power of delay. It can remove obstacles and hindrances in the way of your blessing and rewrite history by making a hedge. It can turn God's wrath away from your city, saving lives from perishing. Do not be afraid. Believe and rise up to God's call. Nehemiah said,

> *"And I looked and rose up, and said unto the nobles, and to the rulers, and to the rest of the people, be not afraid…remember the LORD, which is great and terrible, and fight for your brethren, your sons, and your daughters, your wives and houses" (Nehemiah 4:13).*

Prayer is a shield to our soul, and as the word of God says if we that are called by his name will humble ourselves and confess our sins and pray, he will heal our land. Let God find you worthy and faithful, stand in the gap for your nation, family, and people around you. Many are perishing for there is none to stand in the gap.

SHIELD
OF
FAVOR

God's Shield of Favor is great protection against whatever wants to work contrary.

CHAPTER SEVEN

Shield Of Favor

For You, O Lord, will bless the righteous;
With favor You will surround him as with a
shield (Psalm 5:12).

Favor is a mark of acceptance and approval. Where others are turned back, a carrier of favor will get there and receive approval. May God's favor be a shield around you. Several times I have experienced the favor of God. I can boldly say if it had not been for God's favor, I don't know where I would be today. I remember being at the American Embassy in Nigeria for an interview with my husband. He was the reason we went, but the interviewer just looked at me - heavy, about eight-months pregnant - and said, "You can go and sit down, come next week to collect the visa for you and your child." She then proceeded to ask my husband a series of questions.

Favor is a Spirit; it is an anointing. When rested upon you, like it did on Mary the mother of Jesus, the result will not be natural but supernatural. If the Spirit of favor is over you, like it was in the life of Joseph the favorite son of Jacob, you will be distinguished and whatever you do will prosper *(Genesis 39:2-5)*.

Favor is a Spirit; it is an anointing.

The result will not be natural but supernatural.

As a result of God's favor on Joseph everything he touched prospered, and for his sake the blessing of God was upon the house of his master and all that he had in the house and in the field.

May the favor of God surround you as a with a shield.

A great example of a life with a shield of favor was Esther. The story is of Hadassah, a Hebrew orphan girl raised by her uncle, Mordechai, who later became a queen and is a perfect example of a life surrounded with favor as with a shield. It is nothing but the perfume of favor that caused Esther to be distinguished by everyone who beheld her during the pageant at the palace of the King Ahasuerus.

"And Esther obtained favor in the sight of all them that looked upon her" (Esther 2:15).

The carrier of the shield of favor cannot be turned down, and it is impossible for them to be denied. God's Shield of Favor is great protection against whatever wants to work contrary. At a point in the life of Esther, she had to risk her life to safe her people from the evil sanctions that were decreed against them. It was a difficult task for her to go before the king uninvited, but the thought that many lives are in danger wouldn't allow her to sit back and watch her people perish. She took a bold step to appear before the king and instead of death she obtained favor.

I pray for you; God's Shield of Favor will surround you and all yours; where you have been denied, you shall be called back. No matter how many applied for that position, the favor of God will grant you acceptance before the board of decision makers. You will be their choice, for favor will qualify you.

SHADOW AS A SHIELD

The Lord has promised us that if we take shelter under His shadow, He will deliver us from the snare of the fowler and the deadly pestilence.

CHAPTER EIGHT

Shadow As A Shield

Shadow in this context means a place to take shelter from passing storms or evil disasters. Shadows form when something gets in the way, blocking the light. Though God is invisible, we are still protected by his shadow. His words assure us that

> *"whoever dwells in the secret place of the Most High will abide (take shelter) under the Shadow of the Almighty. I will say of the LORD you are my refuge and fortress my God in whom I trust" (Psalm 91vs.1-3).*

When we come under the shelter of the

Almighty, no matter the evil, disaster, or winds coming after us, it will not come near us. As it was written in ***Genesis 19:8,***

> ***"Don't do anything to these men, for they have come under the protection of my roof."***

The shadow of God Almighty is a great shied for anyone that will trust it. I believe that no matter the evil wind blowing your way, God's shadow will protect you and all yours in Jesus' name.

As I am writing this book, I believe that it isn't a coincidence but for a purpose known by God, that the whole world is in panic over the deadly disease COVID-19. The truth is this deadly disease is killing hundreds daily and is causing fear and panic, but whoever will take shelter under the shadow of the almighty God will escape this evil disaster and deadly disease. The Lord has promised us that if we take shelter under His shadow, He will deliver us from the snare of the fowler and the deadly pestilence. He promised to cover us with His feathers and under

His wings we are taking our refuge; his faithfulness will be our shield. God is faithful, dependable, and powerful. Like a mother hen protects her chicks from prey with her wings, we can depend upon our God any time to protect us from evil disasters and deadly diseases.

We are living in the last days and, while I don't want to be negative, things might not be as before. You and I must be the light in our world to protect our family, church, cities, and nation. The Bible says the shadow of Peter brought healing to as many that came to him *(Acts 5:15).* If the

shadow of Peter heals the sick and the power of God is still the same yesterday, today, and forever more, we must not be afraid but react in faith against anything that wants to challenge our faith.

Christians, we are the light in our world, and we have the solution. Jesus is the answer to the pandemic, and until we look up to Him like the Israelites did in the wilderness when they were bitten by snakes, the problem will remain. Thank God for our government and medical professionals; without the help of God man's labor is in vain. God is counting on us in these last days, to rise and be the light, the shadow against anything that wants to threaten the peace of our family, city, church, and nation. He has put the word in our mouth and promised to protect us as we go about His mission to save the world **(Isaiah 49:2-3).**

What kind of pandemic are you going through? What is bringing fear and panic into your life? Fear is an enemy of faith. I know the doctor's report says there is no more hope for you. It might even be that your marriage is at the brink of breaking and it seems like what you've worked for years is about to crumble. It could even be that your children are causing trouble and forgetting what you have taught them since they were born.

There is hope for you. There is surely light at the

end of the tunnel. You don't have to throw in the towel and give up. God is there with you, even with the fear that wants to grip you away from your faith. The protective shadow of God Almighty is with you. It is not a coincidence that you are reading this book; God ordained it. If you will look up to Him and cry out one more time, He will turn things around just as he did for me in 2002.

After the doctor stopped talking to us and it was looking like all hope for my husband's life was fading away, I remembered God's promise in *Number 21:8*, when as a result of complaining and

murmuring GOD allowed the snake to come into the camp of the Israelites, leading to a great loss. Moses cried to God and was told to make a serpent of bronze. Anyone that was bitten by the snake, if they could look at it, would live. And it was written in the book of *John 3:14-15* that

Christ has been lifted for us who believe in Him.

In any situation, if we will look up to Him, what we are petitioning for is guaranteed. I mean that hopeless person will live, that marriage will experience joy again, and that rebellious child will acknowledge God and change for good. I thank the Lord for the faithfulness of His word - it works. And I trust Him and know it will work for you also. "They look up to Him, and their faces brighten and were not ashamed" (Psalm 34:5). In nothing will you be ashamed, keep your eyes on Him and He will come through for you.

As you are looking onto Jesus, it's important to continue to take refuge in the shadow of God's wings and not to allow the situation you're in to make you lose focus. Psalm 57:1b says

"I will take refuge in the shadow of your

wings until the disaster has passed."

It's just a season and it will surely end. Nothing is permanent but God, so let your faith rise and stay calm in the shadow of His wings. He is the one that rides upon the wings of the wind, so don't run from the wind. This too will pass.

LOOK, I AM DOING A NEW THING

When the almighty God is your shield, it means the creator of heaven and earth is a wall around you.

CHAPTER NINE

Look, I Am Doing
A New Thing

*See, I am doing a new thing! Now its spring
up; do you not perceive it. I am making a way
in the wilderness and streams in the waste
land (Isaiah 43:19).*

When the almighty God is your shield, it means the creator of heaven and earth is a wall around you like the mountain surrounds Jerusalem. Regardless of what is coming, it will have to pass through Him. No wonder He promised,

> *"when you pass through the waters, I will be with you, and when you pass through the rivers, they will not sweep over you. When you walk through the fire, you will not be burned, the flames will not set you ablaze"* *(Isaiah 43:2).*

Life's situations are like waters that rise to rivers and can sweep lives, marriages, and businesses away. It can come like a wildfire that burns everything in its path and takes months or years to quench. But God encourages us not to be afraid of such, for it will have no effect over us. We are not to deny the existence of issues in life, but if we are taking refuge in God they will not harm us but bring forth something new to the glory of God.

Today, I thank God for my husband's situation in 2002. It was a wilderness experience, a season we can't forget. With all the experiences, multiple organ failures, muscles collapsing, skin peeling from his head to toes numerous times, you could not see the effect of it on him if he did not tell you. He is supposed to be using a wheelchair because of a partial stroke on his left side, but when God delivers, He delivers you completely. He made his healing a complete healing. He is a God of wonders. He makes everything new.

One of the nurses that took care of him told him he now has a newborn baby's skin. God did not only give him new skin, but a new kidney. Indeed, God did a new thing in our family. At the end of the storm, he gave us a new vehicle.

We sold our house because we were having financial difficulties - he couldn't work, and I had to stay home to take care of him. But to the glory of God, within a year, God provided me a good job with great benefits and gave us a brand-new house. It was from one new thing to the other. God in His infinite mercy turned our captivity around and made it an experience from glory to glory. It was like a dream;

God filled our mouth with laughter and our tongue with shouts of joy (Psalm 126:1-2).

What happened to us advanced the work of God. Like Paul testifies in the book of Philippians 1:12, (NIV)

"Now I want you to know, brothers and sisters, that what has happened to me has actually served to advance the gospel."

Through it all, God's grace has brought out His purpose in us which is our ministry: Sure Mercies Ministries. Daily, God continues doing new things. It's my prayer that whatever situation you are in now will launch you to your next level. And that which the enemy meant for you for evil will work together for your good. After the experience of the three Hebrew boys in the fiery furnace, the idol worshiper King Nebuchadnezzar praised the God who rescued them, and they also were promoted by him.

Daniel 3:26-30 (NIV)

26 Nebuchadnezzar then approached the

opening of the blazing furnace and shouted, "Shadrach, Meshach and Abednego, servants of the Most High God, come out! Come here!"

So, Shadrach, Meshach and Abednego came out of the fire, 27 and the satraps, prefects, governors and royal advisers crowded around them. They saw that the fire had not harmed their bodies, nor was a hair of their heads singed; their robes were not scorched, and there was no smell of fire on them. 28 Then Nebuchadnezzar said, "Praise be to the God of Shadrach, Meshach and Abednego, who has sent his angel and rescued his servants! They trusted in him and defied the king's command and were willing to give up their lives rather than serve or worship any god except their own God. 29 Therefore I decree that the people of any nation or language who say anything against the God of Shadrach, Meshach and Abednego be cut

> *into pieces and their houses be turned into piles of rubble, for no other god can save in this way."*
>
> *30 Then the king promoted Shadrach, Meshach and Abednego in the province of Babylon.*

Truly, what happened to them advanced the gospel. The heathen King praised their God and then promoted the same people that wouldn't bow to his god a few hours ago. **OUR GOD CAN DO ANYTHING.** He will not fail you, keep trusting in His refuge. He is there as you go through the waters and fire. The rivers of life will not sweep you away and no matter how hot the situation is, you will not be burned. You will come out shining better than when you went into it, and God will definitely be glorified. At the end of it, you will enter a season of unending new things that God will begin in your life.

SHIELD OF FAITH

With the covering of the shield of faith, nothing the enemy throws at you will reach or influence you.

CHAPTER TEN

Shield Of
Faith

Finally, be strong in the Lord and in his mighty power.

11 Put on the full armor of God, so that you can take your stand against the devil's schemes.

12 For our struggle is not against flesh and blood, but against the rulers, against the authorities, against the powers of this dark world and against the spiritual forces of evil in the heavenly realms.

13 Therefore put on the full armor of God, so that when the day of evil comes, you may be able to stand your ground, and after you have done everything, to stand (Ephesians 6:10-13).

Our battle in this world is never against flesh and blood but against the rulers, authorities, and evil forces headed by Satan. To conquer them, we must always depend on God and His armor. Apostle Paul admonishes us to put on the armor of God which is God's Shield. But you can only pick up this armor if you belong to God.

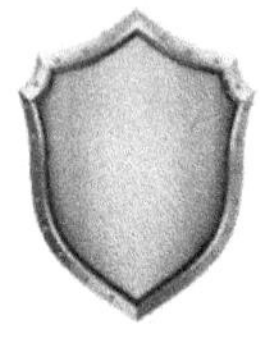

Our battle in this world is never against flesh and blood but against the rulers, authorities, and evil forces headed by Satan.

Our God is a righteous God and cannot behold iniquity, so this armor is for His children. The fourth armor mentioned in *Ephesians* is the shield

of faith. "In addition to all this, take up the shield of faith, with which you can extinguish all the flaming arrows of the evil one". I am glad to let you know that your faith in Christ will annihilate all the arrows of evil against you. According to a teaching of John A. MacMillan, the shield of faith is a protection for the entire body. It represents our complete safety under the blood of Jesus Christ, where no power of the enemy can penetrate.

With the covering of the shield of faith, nothing the enemy throws at you will reach or influence you. I'm always cautious to say, if it's not God sent, it will be God's use. In other words, if you are experiencing anything contrary to God's will, be at peace, it will be for God's use, just as Joseph suffered many evil things before reaching God's destination for him as Egypt's prime minister. He relayed the conclusion of his journey to his brothers, who jumpstarted it by selling him into slavery in Egypt.

> *"You intended to harm me, but God intended it for good to accomplish what is now being done, the saving of many lives" (Genesis 50:20 NIV).*

To withstand the evil day, you must put on the

shield of faith. Faith is simply that you are believing Jesus. God loves the world but hates sin and has made provision to atone the sin of the world.

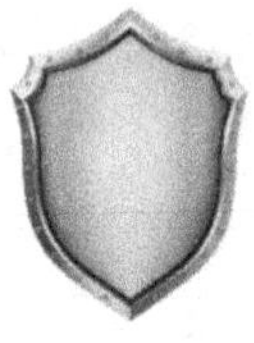 ***With the covering of the shield of faith, nothing the enemy throws at you will reach or influence you.***

To know God, you must first acknowledge that you are a sinner. The book of **Romans 3:23** makes

us know that all have sinned and fallen short of the glory of God. After admitting that you are a sinner, you must believe in the finished work of Christ on the cross to save you, and you must confess Jesus as your LORD and Savior. Once this is done, God will become and continue to be your shield. Without this your sin will prevent Him and expose you to the enemy. You will not be exposed in Jesus' name.

God's protection, provision, security, and preservation are sure when we put on the shield of faith. It's only when we are without the armor that we are exposed to the enemy's attacks. The truth is no one wants to be out of God's Shield, but the Bible warns us that our enemy the devil prowls around like a roaring lion for someone to devour.

"Be alert and of sober mind. Your enemy the devil prowls around like a roaring lion looking for someone to devour. 9 Resist him, standing firm in the faith, because you know that the family of believers throughout the world is undergoing the same kind of sufferings" (1 Peter 5:8-9 NIV).

The adversary of our soul, the devil is going about to lure kingdom people out of God's protection. The devil knows if God remains our shield, he can't do anything against us. This was the situation in the life of Job, a righteous man of faith as described by God *(Job 1:8).* The devil challenged Job's faith by telling God he only fears him because of God's edge (shield of faith) around him. God allowed the devil to touch Job but shielded his soul. He lost everything: his children, businesses, properties - even his wife left him - but in all this he refused to curse God. Job did not sin against God. He was protected, and his end was better than his beginning.

I want to believe that you have accepted Jesus Christ. If not, you can make Him to be your LORD and Savior now and you too will have the access to all His armors, especially the shield of faith. You will be able to extinguish all the flaming arrows of the evil one against you and your family. Most importantly, you will reign with Him at the end of your journey on earth. Life eternal will be your portion in Christ.

Pray This Prayer With Me:

LORD Jesus, I admit that I am a sinner. I believe that you died for my sins on the cross of Calvary. You were buried and rose again to save me from the debt of sin. I ask that you forgive me of all my sins and wash me in your blood. I confess you as my LORD and Savior, I am now your child and you are my LORD and Savior. Thank you, God, for your mercy, grace, love, and the blood of Jesus Christ. I am grateful. In Jesus' name, Amen.

ELIMINATE ANYONE AND ANYTHING THAT WANTS TO BRING YOU OUT OF God's Shield

Now, I want to let you know that Satan will try everything in his power to take you out of God's shield. He will trick and entice you, but he will fail woefully in Jesus' mighty name. To continue to abide under the shelter and enjoy the benefits of having God as your shield, the following must be removed from our lives.

Eliminate the Spirit of Disobedience

To continue to enjoy God's shield and benefits, we must eliminate the spirit of disobedience. The first Adam said,

> **"I heard your voice in the garden, and I was afraid, because I was naked; and I hid myself"**
> **(Gen.3:10 WEB).**

One of Satan's tricks to take the children of God out from under God's shield is to make them deliberately disobey God's commandment.

When one disobeys God, it means the person obeys the devil and becomes the devil's servant. As it is written in the book of

> **Romans 6:16, "You are slaves of the one you obey--whether you are slaves to sin, which leads to death, or to obedience, which leads to righteousness."**

Disobedience to God's instructions is a sin against God and if committed, automatically removes God's shield from the person. After Adam disobeyed God by eating the forbidden fruit, he could not boldly approach God, and the Bible says they were naked and had to cover themselves with leaves. All along God's glory had been their covering, but as soon as they disobeyed the glory was removed and they were covered with shame. God's glory will not be removed from your life and your glory will not turn to shame in Jesus' name.

All that Adam needed, water, food, protection, security, provision, and preservation, was in the garden of Eden, but disobedience took them out of the garden - which is their covering

"Therefore, the Lord God sent him out from the garden of Eden, to cultivate the ground from which he was taken. So, He drove the man out; and at the east of the garden of Eden" (Genesis 3:23-24 NASB).

When God is your shield, He will not only protect you but make daily provision available for you. In God's shield you have security, no fear, and you have preservation, but if the shelter is removed all these are taken. I pray that you will never be naked; the enemy will not turn your glory to shame in Jesus' mighty name. Amen.

Please Pray This Prayer:

Father help me to be obedient to your leading and instructions. Let me never be out of your covering in Jesus' name.

Eliminate Prayerlessness

Prayer is one of the means that God uses to communicate with His children. His word says we should pray without ceasing. There's a story of a man that exercised this instruction in the Bible. Daniel's way of abiding under the shield of the mighty God was through prayer, and the enemy understood this and tried to instigate the power of the land against him. To them that was the only way they could take him out of the shield of God's protection.

At this, the administrators and the satraps tried to find grounds for charges against Daniel in his conduct of government affairs, but they were unable to do so. They could find no corruption in him, because he was trustworthy and neither corrupt nor negligent. Finally, these men said, 'We will never find grounds for charges against Daniel in his conduct of government affairs, but they were unable to do so. They could find no corruption in him, because he was trustworthy and neither corrupt nor negligent. Finally, these men said,

> *We will never find any basis for charges against this man Daniel unless it has something to do with the law of his God"*
> *(Daniel 6:4-5).*

It is important to know that the goal of the enemy is to take us out of God's shield so he can attack. The enemy knows that if they make Daniel sin against the commandment of God, it will be easy to touch him. They asked the king to decree that no one should pray to any god or man for thirty days except to the king, and whoever violated this law should be thrown into the lion den *(Daniel 6:7-9).*

Despite the consequence for breaking the king's rule, Daniel would not compromise his faith and beliefs. He observed his prayer like he usually did.

"Now Daniel so distinguished himself among the administrators and the satraps by his exceptional qualities that the king planned to set him over the whole kingdom.10 Now when Daniel learned that the decree had been published, he went home to his upstairs room where the windows opened toward Jerusalem. Three times a day he got down on his knees and prayed, giving thanks to his God, just as he had done before"

(Daniel 6:3 & 10).

Wherever you are today, you got there through prayer, and it will take prayer to sustain it. Daniel knew it was by the power of God that he attained the president position and it would take God to keep him in the position.

Don't allow prayerlessness to eliminate you from the position in which God has placed you. Whether you're the president of a company, mother, business owner, Pastor, Bishop, wife, the list goes on, you are what you are by the power of His grace, and it will take God's grace to sustain you in that position. A lot of us have gone many days of prayer and fasting before we achieved our success, but now that we have been lifted, we are too busy to pray.

To stay in His presence for an hour is difficult; we justify our busyness by claiming that God understands. Some even prefer to pay a pastor or a prophet to pray for them than to spend quality time with the source and the sustained of their miracle. Hide your family, business, job, children, and whatever you have gotten in the place of prayer under the shadow of the Lord and keep watch and pray over them. You will not fall prey to the tricks of the enemy.

Eliminate the Spirit of Pride

According to the New Strong's Expanded Exhaustive Concordance Bible, pride is a conceited sense of one's superiority. It is originated from the Devil and hinders us from coming to God.

"Though the LORD be high, yet hath he respects unto the lowly: but the proud he knows afar off" (Psalm 138:6).

The almighty God our shield cannot behold iniquity. Pride is a sin and God deals with proud people from afar off. To abide under the shelter of the almighty God, one must be humble. Humility pays off because it allows you to enjoy the presence of GOD. In His presence is the fullness and at His right hand is pleasure forever.

Satan used to be the head of the angels of God and dwelled in His presence until pride entered him, and this resulted in him being cast away from God's presence onto the earth.

He said in his heart,

"I will ascend to the heaven; I will raise my throne above the stars of God; I will sit enthroned on the mount of assembly, on the utmost heights of Mount Zaphon. I will

ascend above the tops of the clouds; I will make myself like the Most High. But you are brought down to the realm of the dead, to the depths of the pit" (Isaiah 14:13-15).

Pride does not only bring a person down but separates one from God. I pray no matter how high God lifts you, you will not allow the spirit of pride in your life. You will not fall but continue to move from glory to glory, for everyone that appears in His presence will go from strength to strength

(Psalm 84:7). The presence of God will forever be your shield.

I pray to God to keep your soul, spirit, and body from the greatest enemy of man, Satan. If you have given your life to Christ, the spirit of disobedience and pride will not have their place in your life. You will not be tired but keep moving forward in Him, and God will preserve you till the end.

It does not matter which kind of wilderness you may be going through, stand firm in your faith in God and His word and He will surely help you through. He did not promise that it will be easy, but He promises to not leave you or forsake you. With perseverance you will make it if you don't quit. "By perseverance snail reach the ark"; you will reach your destination.

My Husband's Testimony

Absolutely nothing is impossible for our God. You just have to believe. Be blessed as you read from the horse's mouth.

Jeremiah 1:5 says: "Before I formed thee in the belly, I knew thee; and before thou camest forth out of the womb I sanctified thee, and I ordained thee a prophet unto the nations."

I was born to a Christian family in Nigeria, West Africa. I majored in Religious Studies and Philosophy after which I migrated to the United States of America with my wife, Fehintola, and our daughter, Toluwanimi, in 1998 as a missionary by the leading of the Lord. We joined a Christ-believing church in Houston, Texas, where we served the Lord wholeheartedly for ten years, during which the Lord blessed us with a son, Oluwadamilola.

I was hale and hearty all my life until January 2002 when the enemy struck with his ministry – to steal, kill, and destroy (John 10:10). I was fasting, seeking the face of the Lord for His next assignment for my life and family for the new year. Towards the end of the fasting; I was diagnosed with LYMPHOMA T-CELL (cancer of the blood).

The sickness worsened until I was fully admitted into the hospital. After a series of medical examinations and without any medication or chemotherapy, Jehovah Rapha (My Healer) cancelled the report of the enemy; the bible says "By whose (Christ) stripes ye were healed" (1 Peter 2:24). All the medical staff was astonished at the turn of events, but still I was very sick without a diagnosis. The lead doctor was pressured to proffer a solution, and he sincerely said to the brethren that surrounded my family at that crucial season of my life, "but I am not God"; his words passed a clear message across to them that only God can intervene in this case.

The sickness persisted to the extent that I went into a coma and for a period of almost three months I was on life support. News went around that I was actually dead; some said I had a terminal disease and others said it was the highest stage of HIV.

Proverb 19:21 says, "There are many devices in a man's heart nevertheless the counsel of the Lord shall stand."

By the time I came out of the coma, the doctors said the left side of my brain had shut down forever, and even if I ever made it out of the hospital I would never function as a human being, nor be able to walk again. During that period all organs in my body shut down, which the doctors called "Multiple Organ Failure" (the heart, kidney, lungs, and muscles failed - even my skin from head to my toe peeled five times).

After all medical knowledge failed, what the doctors knew to be medically impossible was made possible: I was healed. The Bible says in *Mathew 19:26 "…with men this is impossible; but with God all things are possible."*

I am a living testimony to this word, for all organs that failed are functioning perfectly well to the glory of God.

Today, I am perfectly healed. I now travel all over the world to preach the gospel of our Lord Jesus Christ and share my testimony to every ear that listens. This testimony has given birth unto greater testimonies, and my prayer is that as you read, you will have a greater testimony today.

Sure Mercies Ministries (SMM) was born from the faithfulness of the Lord towards me and my family, the fulfillment of the vow we made, and covenant we made with God to serve Him all the rest of our lives, and since the ministry began it has been from glory to glory. Please share your testimony and comments with us today, we shall surely rejoice with you.

You are also welcomed to fellowship with us in Houston Texas anytime you are in town.
"Ye also may have fellowship with us: and truly our fellowship is with the Father and with His Son Jesus Christ" (1 John 1:3).

Toyin John Ayoola (Pastor)